STEPS
TO INDEPENDENT LIVING

THIRD EDITION

How to Take Care of Your Home

Nancy Lobb

illustrated by David Strauch

WALCH EDUCATION

Certified Chain of Custody
Promoting Sustainable
Forest Management

www.sfiprogram.org

SGS-SFI/COC-US09/5501

1   2   3   4   5   6   7   8   9   10

ISBN 978-0-8251-6497-2

Contents

Part 3: Keeping Washable Goods Clean

To the Student

Living on your own can be a great experience! You can choose and decorate your own place. You can decide for yourself what and when to eat. You can set your own hours. In short, you are free to make your own choices about your lifestyle.

Along with these freedoms comes responsibility. Living on your own means it's up to you to take care of yourself when you're sick or hurt. You are now the one who must be sure your nutritional, physical, and emotional needs are met. No one will be watching over you to ensure your personal safety. No one will be looking to make sure you make good decisions about alcohol, drugs, and tobacco. It's up to you!

But that's not all! You must make good choices as you choose and set up your home. You must keep your home safe and clean. And you must use your money wisely to meet your needs.

You will have a better experience living on your own if you are prepared to meet your new responsibilities. The six books in the *Steps to Independent Living* series will teach you the skills you need to make it on your own.

In this book, *How to Take Care of Your Home,* you will learn about:

- safety in the home

- keeping your home clean

- keeping washable goods clean

We hope this information helps prepare you for the day you start living on your own!

www.walch.com

Self-Test

How much do you know about keeping a home safe and clean?
Circle YES or NO for each question.

1. Do you know how to put out a grease fire safely?

   YES   NO

2. Do you know what to do if you're trapped by a fire?

   YES   NO

3. Do you know how to protect children from poisoning?

   YES   NO

4. Can you use electrical appliances safely?

   YES   NO

5. Do you know what to do if your gas stove leaks?

   YES   NO

6. Do you know how to keep out burglars?

   YES   NO

7. Do you know how to prevent food poisoning?

   YES   NO

8. Do you know how to save time cleaning your house?

   YES   NO

9. Do you know how to choose laundry products?

   YES   NO

Continued

www.walch.com

10. Do you know how to wash clothing correctly?

    YES   NO

11. Can you dry clothes so they don't shrink and wrinkle?

    YES   NO

12. Do you know how to use a washer and dryer safely?

    YES   NO

13. Do you know how to use a space heater safely?

    YES   NO

14. Do you know what to do if a circuit breaker keeps tripping?

    YES   NO

15. Do you know where to put smoke detectors in your home?

    YES   NO

16. Do you know how to choose a safe throw rug?

    YES   NO

17. Do you know how to keep a sliding door safely shut?

    YES   NO

How many YES answers did you have? _____

After you read this book, take the self-test again.

How many YES answers did you have this time? _____

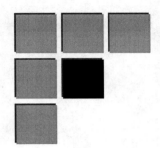

PART 1

Keep It Safe!

Fire Prevention

No one likes to think about a fire in the home. But every year many homes go up in flames. Protect yourself and your family. Know what to do to prevent fire.

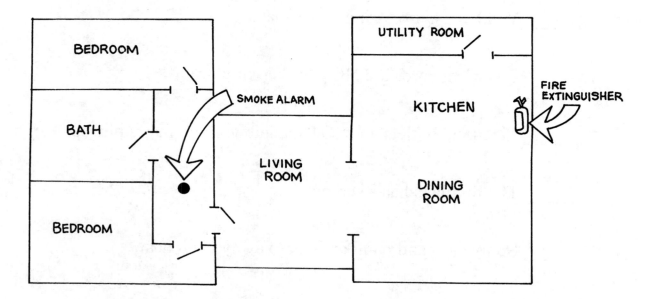

Look at the picture above. Then answer the questions.

1. Where is the fire extinguisher? Explain why the fire extinguisher is placed there.

2. Where is the smoke detector? Explain why the smoke detector is placed there.

www.walch.com

Now think about your own home. Use the checklist below to show what you find.

_____ You have smoke detectors that work.

_____ You have a fire extinguisher that works.

_____ Electrical cords are NOT broken or worn.

_____ Electrical outlets are NOT loaded with too many plugs.

_____ The fireplace has a screen.

_____ Spray cans and paint are stored away from heat.

_____ Electrical cords DO NOT run under rugs.

_____ No flammable things are near the furnace, hot-water heater, or space heater.

_____ Space heaters are NOT used with extension cords.

Continued ➤

_____ There is air space around the TV, stereo, computer, lamps, and so on.

_____ The lint screen on the clothes dryer is kept clean.

_____ Matches and lighters are stored out of children's reach.

_____ Gas and/or oil are in approved safety containers away from heat and outside the house.

More Fire Prevention

Fireplaces, furnaces, and space heaters are great sources of warmth during cold weather. If you use any one of these heat sources, be sure to read and follow directions for proper use. Also, a few simple steps will ensure you are safe from accidental fire.

Fireplaces

Always use a fireplace screen to keep the fire in the fireplace. Never store matches, kindling, or newspapers near the fireplace. Chimneys should be inspected yearly and cleaned when needed. If you have a gas fireplace, light the match before you turn on the gas.

Furnaces/Heaters

Furnaces should be inspected every year. Never store flammable items on or near a furnace or hot-water heater.

Turn off the space heater when you leave the room. Don't use an extension cord with a space heater. Make sure the space heater is not close to anything flammable. If you have a gas space heater, light the match before you turn on the gas.

Clothes Dryer

Clean the lint trap every time you use the dryer. Never leave your home with the dryer running.

www.walch.com

Electrical Appliances

You might be surprised to learn that many home fires are caused by misuse of electrical appliances, overloading circuits, or simply not keeping appliances clean.

It's best not to use extension cords. If you do use one, make sure it's in good shape. Never run an extension cord under a rug. Never loop it around a nail or hook.

Check your wall outlets. An outlet that is loose or has hanging wires should be repaired by an electrician. Don't plug a lot of items into the same outlet.

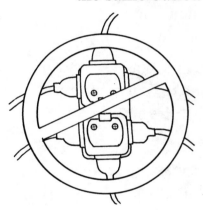

If you have a fuse or circuit breaker that keeps tripping, you may have too many things plugged in to that line. Unplug one or more appliances.

Check lamps and light fixtures to see what type of bulb they should use. Don't use bulbs that have a wattage that is too high for that fixture.

When you buy an appliance, check to see that it has the UL (Underwriters Laboratories) label. This means it has met approved safety standards.

Smoke Detectors

Many people in the United States die in house fires each year. Nearly half of these fires happen while families are asleep. Three-quarters of the deaths are due to smoke inhalation. You can see why it is important to have smoke detectors in your home.

Make sure there is a smoke detector on every floor of your home. If you live in a small home on one level, you will need one smoke detector. It should be located outside your bedroom close to the kitchen area.

If you live in a multi-story house or apartment building, make sure there is at least one smoke detector on each floor. These should be in hallways and outside of the bedrooms.

Of course, it doesn't do much good to have a smoke detector that doesn't work. You should test each smoke detector once a month. There is a test button you can press. If the smoke detector is working, the alarm will sound.

Replace the battery in your smoke detector at least once a year. If you hear a chirping sound, that means the battery needs to be replaced.

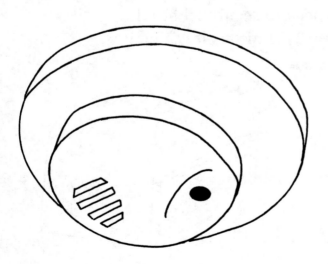

You should also keep the smoke detector free from dust or dirt.

If you are renting an apartment, a smoke detector should be provided for you. If not, they are not expensive to buy. Your local fire station may have free smoke detectors available at certain times of the year.

                                                   www.walch.com

Putting Out a Small Fire

You are the most important thing in your house. Don't hurt yourself trying to put out a big or fast-growing fire. Get out fast! Call the fire department from a neighbor's home. But you can put out a very small fire without putting yourself in danger. Just use good sense!

A fire extinguisher should be located in your kitchen. A multi-purpose (also known as an ABC) extinguisher works on almost all types of fires. Learn how to use the fire extinguisher <u>before</u> there is a fire. Read the directions and make sure you understand them. Remember, never try to use a fire extinguisher on a large fire. Get out and call 911 instead.

Here is what you can do in case of some common small fires:

1. **Fire in a pan**

   Put the lid on.

   Turn off the stove.

2. **Grease fire**

   DO NOT use water! (The fire might splash up in your face.)

   Cover the pan with the lid.

   OR Pour baking soda or salt on the pan.

   Turn off the stove.

www.walch.com

3. **Fire in the oven**

   Turn off the oven.

   Keep the door shut to
   keep the fire inside.

4. **Fire in a wastebasket**

   Put water on it.

5. **Electrical fire**

   DO NOT use water!

   Pull out the plug
   (if you can do so safely).

   Use a fire extinguisher.

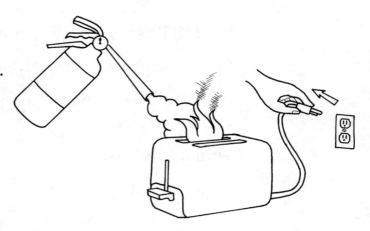

Escaping a Home Fire

If a fire is too big for you to put out easily, get out of the home. Be sure everyone leaves. Call the fire department from a neighbor's home. Don't go back inside to save things.

If there is a lot of smoke in the home, crawl on the floor to the exit. The air near the floor will be clearer.

Touch a closed door before you open it. If it's hot, fire is on the other side. Find another way out.

If you live in a tall building that has an elevator, never use the elevator during a fire. Take the stairs. Read the building evacuation plan. Know how to get out of the building.

If you're trapped by a fire, get by a window. Open the window just a crack for air. Hang something (like a sheet) out the window to attract attention. Stuff something under the door to keep out smoke.

If your clothes catch fire, **STOP, DROP,** and **ROLL.**

STOP—Don't run for help!

DROP to the floor.

ROLL on the floor over and over until the fire is out.

www.walch.com

Be prepared. Have a family fire drill. Here are some things you should do to prepare:

1. Plan ways to escape from each room in your home in case of fire. Make sure everyone knows what to do.

2. Half of all home fires happen at night. Be sure to sleep with your door closed. If there is a fire, that will hold it back. If your bedroom door feels hot, don't open it. Exit through a window or another door.

3. If your bedroom is on the second floor or higher, have a window escape ladder. These are made to use in case of fire.

4. Decide on a place to meet outside so you'll know everyone is safe.

5. Call 911 from another location.

6. Make sure no one goes back inside to rescue anything!

Check Yourself

Read each statement below. If the person did the right thing, write YES. If not, write NO. Explain each NO answer.

_____ 1. Mr. and Mrs. Baez had a family fire drill.

_____ 2. Mrs. Brown had a grease fire on her stove. She quickly poured a pitcher of water on it.

_____ 3. There was a fire at the Adams's house. Mr. Adams called the fire department. Then he woke up his family.

_____ 4. Ari's sleeve caught on fire. He ran quickly to get help.

_____ 5. Erin's toaster caught on fire. She threw water on it.

_____   6. Mr. Lind stored gasoline on a high shelf over the heater. It was out of the reach of children.

_____   7. Lila ran lamp cords under the rug to hide them.

_____   8. There was a fire in a pan. Andre put the lid on.

_____   9. The house was on fire. There was a lot of smoke. Maria stood up, hoping to breathe the least smoke.

_____   10. There was a fire in the house. Ramon touched the bedroom door. It was hot, so he went out the window.

Preventing Poisoning

You probably know that a skull and crossbones means poison! But not all poisons are marked with this symbol or with the word "poison."

Many cleaners and medicines used in the home can be poisonous if used in the wrong way. Small children are most often the victims of poisoning.

Be safe! Follow these rules.

Medicines

- Store medicines in locked cabinets out of children's reach.

- Buy products with childproof lids. (But remember, children may still be able to get these open.)

- Leave products in the containers in which they were bought. Never pour them into a different bottle.

- Follow directions on medicine labels exactly. Don't guess.

- Never tell a child that medicine tastes like candy.

- Get rid of expired medicines. Take them out of their containers. Mix them with a substance such as used coffee grounds or kitty litter. Put this mixture in a sealed container and throw it in the trash can outside.

www.walch.com

Cleaning Products

- Don't store cleaners under the sink.

- Don't store cleaners, automotive products, or gardening products in the same cabinet with your food.

- Never put cleaners in containers that once held food or drinks.

- Store cleaners and sprays in a high cabinet.

- Buy safety latches for cabinets containing cleaners if you have small children.

- While you are cleaning the house, don't leave buckets containing cleaners out if a child is around.

- Read and follow directions on household cleaners.

Other Items

- Never eat food that looks or smells bad.

- Teach children not to eat things they find without asking. Many berries, leaves, and mushrooms are poisonous.

- Keep alcoholic drinks where children or pets cannot reach them.

- Keep automotive products and gardening products out of children's and pets' reach.

- Keep cosmetics and toiletries out of children's and pets' reach. Perfume, hair dye, hair spray, shoe polish, and nail polish can all be harmful.

In case of poisoning:

Get help fast! Call 911. Or call the toll-free Poison Control Center number: 1-800-222-1222.

Safety with Electricity

Electricity does great things for us. It makes life easier and more convenient—but it can be a killer, too. Use electricity with care. Here are some guidelines to follow:

- Don't use electricity near water or in wet areas.

- Never use an electrical appliance while standing on a wet floor.

- If an appliance gets wet, turn off the power supply. Then unplug the appliance. Don't plug it in again until you have inspected it and it has dried.

- Don't clean a plugged-in appliance with anything metal.

- Don't use an appliance with a broken cord.

- Don't let children play with electrical appliances.

- Don't plug too many things into the same outlet.

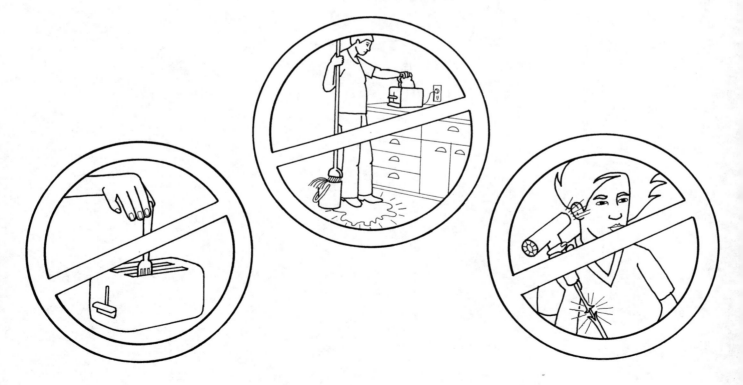

- If an extension cord feels warm, it is not safe to use. Use outside cords for outside jobs.

- Large appliances must be grounded. Use three-pronged outlets for three-pronged plugs.

- Never go near a downed power line. Never touch a downed power line even if it appears to be safe. Call the power company.

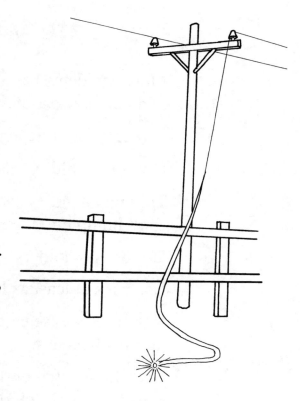

- If someone is being electrocuted, don't touch the person with your hands or anything metal. Use a dry wooden pole or wooden broomstick to push the person away from the electrical source. Turn off the power if you can.

- Stay out of floodwaters. They may be hiding power lines or other dangers. If floodwater enters your home, turn off your electricity at the fuse box or circuit box by flipping the master switch.

Safety in the Kitchen

More accidents happen in the kitchen than in any other room of a home. Most of these are burns, cuts, or falls.

To keep your kitchen safe, follow these rules:

1. Don't let children play near a hot stove.

2. Turn pan handles back from the edge of the stove so you can't bump into them.

3. Use dry potholders.

4. Use pans at least as large as the burner you plan to use.

5. Hot oil or grease catch fire easily. If oil or grease smokes, turn the heat down.

6. Keep things that burn (such as paper and boxes) off the stovetop. They could catch fire.

7. Don't store things that can catch fire easily near any hot appliances. This includes towels, pot holders, and bags of food.

8. Don't cook wearing long, loose sleeves. They could brush against the burner and catch fire. Avoid reaching across the stove for anything while cooking.

9. If you smell gas from your gas stove, open the window. Don't light a match. Call the gas company.

10. Keep a fire extinguisher in or near the kitchen. Know how to use it.

11. Don't use kitchen appliances that have worn or damaged cords.

12. Keep appliances, including the stove and exhaust fan, clean and free from grease.

13. Never operate an empty microwave oven.

14. Never leave your cooking unattended.

Preventing Falls

Injuries caused by falls are common. Use your common sense to prevent falls. Here are some ideas to get you started:

- If you have stairs, keep them free of clutter. Be sure they are well lit. Sturdy railings are a must. Non-skid material on the steps is important, too.

- Don't fall in the dark! Have a light by your bed. Have a light switch at the entrance to each room.

- Improve the lighting in your home. Make sure each room is adequately lit.

- Keep sidewalks shoveled in the winter. Apply sand or salt to ice that is too hard to remove.

- Wipe up spills right away. They might cause you to slip.

- Remove throw rugs or be sure they have a non-skid backing.

- Put a non-skid mat or stickers in the bathtub.

- Arrange furniture so you're not likely to fall over it.

- Keep loose objects such as toys, tools, shoes, and papers off the floor.

- Keep items you use often in cabinets you can reach without using a step stool or ladder.

- Use ladders or sturdy stools for climbing.

Under Lock and Key

To help keep your home safe from burglars, make it hard to break into. Most burglars will look for an easier target. Here are some ways to keep burglars out:

- Lock the doors at night and when you go out. Use a dead bolt lock.

- Use a chain on the door.

- Brace sliding doors shut from the inside. Put a metal rod in the track of the door. Cut a piece of wood to make a brace.

- Lock all windows when they're shut.

- Don't put valuables near windows where they are easily seen.

- Engrave your name on items such as bicycles and TVs.

- Put jewelry or small valuables where they won't be easily found.

- When you go out, make it look as if someone is still home. Leave some lights on and a radio playing.

- Get a dog.

- Don't keep a lot of money in your home.

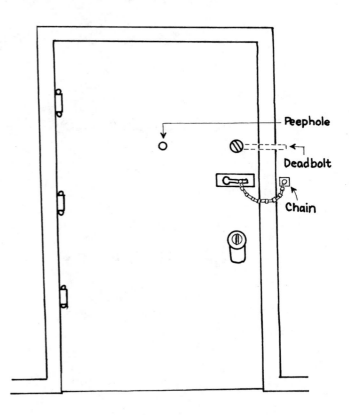

What Would You Do?

Tell what you would do in each situation below.

1. Bread is stuck in the toaster.

2. You need a new lock on your front door.

3. The cord on the vacuum cleaner is broken. You need to vacuum.

4. You have a gas stove. You notice a strong smell of gas one day.

5. You are using an extension cord. It feels hot.

www.walch.com

6. A child you are taking care of drinks some household cleaner.

7. A storm has downed a power line in your yard.

8. You need to get rid of some old medicine.

9. Someone is being electrocuted.

10. You are heating some oil. It catches fire.

11. You are shopping for a new throw rug for your kitchen floor.

12. You are worried about someone forcing open your sliding door.

13. A circuit breaker in your home keeps tripping.

14. You are shopping for a new microwave. You find one on sale that does not have the UL label on it.

True or False?

Write TRUE or FALSE on the line in front of each statement that follows. If it is false, explain why.

_____ 1. All products that can cause poisoning are marked "poison."

_____ 2. A good place to store leftover cleaner is in a soft-drink bottle with a tight lid.

_____ 3. Don't waste food just because it smells a bit "off."

_____ 4. All kids eat leaves and berries. Don't worry about it.

_____ 5. Chains on doors have no safety value.

Continued ➡

_____ 6. When you go out at night, turn out all the lights and lock the doors.

_____ 7. It's best to carry all your money with you.

_____ 8. If you have a three-pronged cord that won't fit the outlet, cut off the third prong.

_____ 9. Be sure pans are much smaller than the burner you're using.

_____ 10. Avoid non-skid backings on throw rugs.

www.walch.com

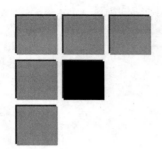

PART 2

Keep It Clean!

You Don't Have to Eat Off the Floor!

Some people like their homes to be spotless. Others have no interest at all in keeping things clean. Who's right? Does keeping things clean matter? Does a little dirt hurt anyone?

Well, yes and no. Each person must decide how clean is clean enough. But there are reasons for keeping things at least somewhat clean.

A dirty bathroom is full of germs. It may smell bad, too. Clean the bathroom well at least once a week. Use disinfectant to kill germs.

Food fixed in a dirty kitchen may look good but be very bad for you. Food poisoning can result if food handling areas are not kept clean. So, keep the kitchen clean! Wash dishes and take out the trash daily. Keep work surfaces wiped up.

Spiders, roaches, silverfish, and other pests love dirty corners. They carry dirt and germs all over your home. To get rid of them, keep things clean. You may need to use bug sprays as well. Or, hire a pest control service.

Living in dirt and clutter can make you feel unsettled. A clean, orderly home is more pleasant.

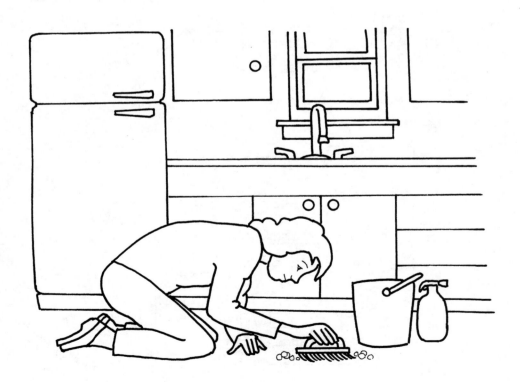

Make It Easy on Yourself!

No one wants to spend a lot of time cleaning. Don't spend more time than you need to. Save your time for things you enjoy. Here are a few ways to get the most done for the least work.

- Have a place for everything. Keep everything in its place.

- Keep things neat as you go. When you're done using something, put it away. Hang up clothes when you take them off. Wash dirty dishes after each meal. (Or put them in the dishwasher.) Leave the bathroom neat after each time you use it.

- Put a doormat by each outside door. This keeps dirt outside, not inside!

- Have a spot for your cleaning supplies. Keep everything you use on hand.

- Set up a schedule for cleaning. You might do one job each day. Or you might pick one day to do all the cleaning.

- Before you start any cleaning project, gather all your supplies. Stopping to find cleansers or sponges will eat up your time.

Cleaning Tools and Supplies

Look for the cleaning supply aisle in any grocery store or home-supply store. You'll find a huge number of products to choose from! Many of these cost a lot and are not needed. But some may save you time. You must decide if they are worth the extra money.

What do you really need to keep a clean house? Let's take a look at the basics.

Cleaning Tools

- broom
- dustpan
- dust mop
- dust cloths
- scrub brush

- wet mop
- pail
- toilet brush
- sponges
- vacuum (if you have carpets)

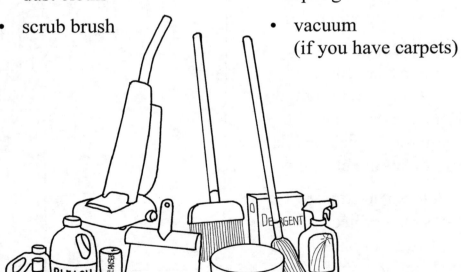

Cleaning Supplies

- powdered cleanser
- disinfectant
- detergent
- dishwashing soap
- furniture polish/spray
- liquid cleaner
- glass cleaner

* Never mix cleaners. Chlorine bleach and ammonia combine to form a toxic gas that can kill you.

Cleaning the Kitchen

Everyone has his or her own way to clean a room. The list below is a suggested cleaning plan. You may want to do a job more or less often than is suggested here.

Daily or After Each Use

- Put away leftovers.
- Wash and put away dishes.
- Wash sink.
- Wipe counters and table.
- Sweep floor.
- Empty garbage.

Weekly

- Throw out old food.
- Wipe out refrigerator.
- Wash stove burners.
- Wash floors.

Sometimes/As Needed

- Wash curtains or blinds.

- Wash walls.

- Clean out cabinets.

- Wipe down and clean out drawers.

- Clean oven.

- Clean refrigerator well.

- Wipe down small appliances such as toaster and mixer.

- Wipe cabinet fronts.

- Dust and clean ceiling fan and items hanging on the wall.

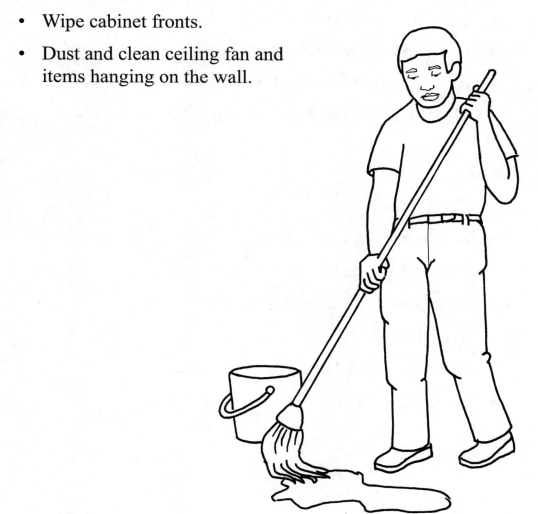

Cleaning the Bathroom

To keep a bathroom free of germs and odors, you must clean it often. Here is a schedule for cleaning the bathroom. You may choose to do a task more or less often.

Daily

- Rinse sinks.
- Wipe the mirror and faucets.
- Wipe down the shower door.
- Hang up towels and washcloths.
- Replace dirty towels and washcloths.
- Place any dirty clothing in hamper, basket, or laundry room.

Weekly

- Wash floor.
- Scrub toilet with disinfectant.
- Scrub sinks and tub.
- Scrub shower and shower curtain.
- Wash mirror.
- Empty wastebaskets.
- Vacuum/shake out rug.

Sometimes/As Needed

- Wash windows.

- Wash rug.

- Clean out cabinets.

- Dust ceiling, vents, and fans.

- Wash curtains and blinds.

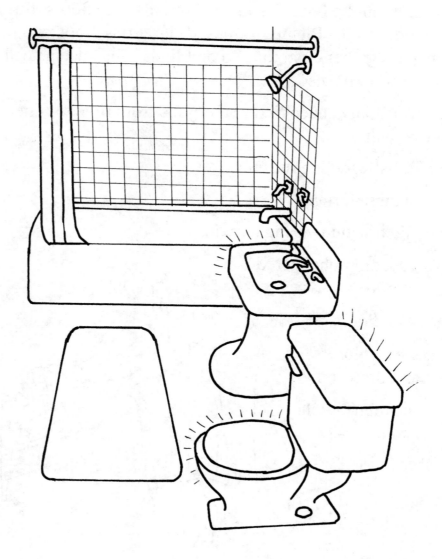

Cleaning Other Rooms

Here are some cleaning guidelines. You may want to do a job more or less often than is suggested here.

Some jobs need to be done daily. Making beds is one of these. Picking up clutter is another. If you let stuff pile up all week, cleaning it up turns into a huge job!

Dusting and vacuuming must be done weekly. Dust gets on everything in the house! You need to dust bare floors, furniture, and window sills. Picture frames, decorations, TVs, and other electronics gather dust, too. So do blinds. Bed sheets need to be changed weekly, also.

You'll also need to do other jobs from time to time. A few of these include:

- Polish wooden furniture.

- Shampoo rugs.

- Wash windows and curtains.

- Vacuum upholstered furniture.

- Wax floors.

- Clean closets and drawers.

- Vacuum couches and chairs.

Using Cleaners Safely

Many household cleaners contain strong chemicals. Always read the label before using a cleaner. Follow the directions. Never mix chemicals. Chlorine bleach and ammonia mix to make a toxic gas that can kill.

Read the label below. Then answer the questions that follow.

Drainie Drain Cleaner
**POISON. CONTAINS LYE. CAUSES SEVERE EYE DAMAGE. MAY CAUSE BLINDNESS.
WILL CAUSE INTERNAL BURNS IF SWALLOWED.
KEEP DRAINIE AWAY FROM SKIN, EYES,
AND CLOTHING.**
Keep away from children.

FIRST AID
Eyes: Flood with water for 20 minutes. Seek medical help.

If swallowed: Give large amounts of milk or water.
Do not induce vomiting. Seek medical help.

Skin: Flood with water for 15 minutes.
Seek medical help for burns.

---

1. Where should Drainie be stored?

www.walch.com

2.   What happens if you swallow Drainie?

3.   What could Drainie do to your eyes?

4.   What should you do if Drainie gets in your eyes?

5.   What should you do if someone swallows Drainie?

6.   What should you do if you get Drainie on your hands?

Check Yourself

1. Why is it important to keep a kitchen clean?

2. List two reasons for keeping a bathroom clean.

   a.

   b.

3. Why are bugs such as roaches unhealthy to have around?

4. Name three daily jobs in keeping a kitchen clean.

   a.

   b.

   c.

Continued

www.walch.com

5. How can you kill germs in a bathroom?

6. List two ways to get rid of bugs in your house.
    a.

    b.

7. List two reasons to read labels on household cleaners.
    a.

    b.

8. Explain why you should never mix products containing ammonia and chlorine bleach.

Continued

9. List five ways to reduce the amount of time you need to spend cleaning.

    a.

    b.

    c.

    d.

    e.

10. List five cleaning tools and five cleaners you think would be most useful.

	Tools	Cleaners
a.		
b.		
c.		
d.		
e.		

PART 3

Keeping Washable
Goods Clean

The Basics

Clothes and washable household goods cost a lot. Learn to take care of them the right way. They'll last longer and look better. Here are a few basics:

- After you wear something, put it in the wash if it's dirty. If it's not dirty, hang it up or fold it.

- Protect your clothes from spills. Use napkins, aprons, or coveralls to keep clothes clean.

- If you do spill something, get the spot out as soon as you can. The longer a stain "sets," the harder it will be to get out. Don't ever iron a stain. The heat will "set" the stain.

- When you wash, be careful. Use the right water temperature. Use the right amount of detergent.

- Brush items that need dry cleaning as needed to get rid of dirt and lint. Store clean wool items in sealed plastic bags or boxes during the summer to keep out moths.

Reading Labels

Clothes, sheets, and curtains can be made of many types of fabric. Each type of fabric needs a different kind of cleaning. If you wash something the wrong way, it may shrink, fade, or just not come clean.

How do you know how to wash each item? It's easy! Just read the label.

Read each label that follows. Write YES if the person followed the directions. Write NO if the person did not.

A Wool Rug

1. Jae took her rug to the dry-cleaners. She had it dry-cleaned.

   _____

   **Dry Clean
   Only**

2. Owen put his rug in a coin-operated dry-cleaning machine.

   _____

3. Aisha washed and dried her rug at the Laundromat.

   _____

Continued ➡

www.walch.com

Kitchen Curtains

4. Marta washed her curtains. She let them sit in the dryer for 30 minutes after the dryer had stopped.

_____

```
┌─────────────────────┐
│  Machine Wash        │
│      Warm            │
│  Tumble Dry          │
│  Remove              │
│  Promptly            │
└─────────────────────┘
```

5. John had his curtains dry-cleaned.

_____

6. Mario washed his curtains in warm water. Then he put them in the dryer.

_____

All About Laundry Products

Many stores have a whole aisle full of laundry products. Which ones do you need? To decide, you must learn a little about what each one does.

Product	Its Job and Features
Detergent	Cleans fabrics Works in all types of water Good cleaning power Can be used in hot or cold water May have bleach, softener, or scent
Soap	Cleans fabrics Works best in soft water Gentle on fabrics Best for baby clothes and hand-washables Works best in hot or warm water
Bleach	Whitens white fabrics Removes many stains Deodorizes

Product	Its Job and Features
Fabric softener	Softens clothes Works in all types of water Reduces static cling
Water conditioner	Softens hard water Prevents soap scum in hard water
Starch	Makes fabric look crisp when ironed
Stain remover	Comes in spray, powder, or liquid form May be put on stains before washing

www.walch.com

Doing the Wash

Using a washing machine is not hard. But being aware of a few simple rules will help you get better results.

- Read the label on each item to see if it's washable. If you're not sure, wait and ask someone.

- Sort the items to be washed by color. Whites go in one load. Colors go in another.

- If a colored item is new, wash it by itself the first time. If you don't, the color may run onto another item.

- Treat stains before you wash.

- Follow directions on the detergent box. Measure detergent carefully. Don't use more than you need. Don't use too little, either.

How hard can this be? Just dump it all in. Add detergent. Add bleach and go!

- Prepare clothing for washing. Close zippers and other fasteners. Empty pockets. Remove unwashable belts or trims.

- Be careful if you use bleach. Don't use more than the directions say. Also, don't pour bleach right on fabric. The bleach could put holes in the fabric.

Using the Washing Machine

First, measure the detergent. Put it in the tub first. Then add sorted clothes. Fill the tub loosely. Don't try to jam in too many items.

Set the water level to match the load size. Choose hot, warm, or cold water. You only need hot water for very dirty items. You'll save money by choosing warm or cold wash water. Cold water is fine for the rinse cycle.

You can decide what type of washing action you prefer. Regular or normal is best for everything except delicate items.

Wash time can be set from just a few minutes to much longer. Choose the wash time based on how dirty the items are.

Spin speed can be normal or gentle. You will usually want to choose normal spin. It removes the most water from the clothing so you won't have to dry the clothes as long. Use gentle on delicate items.

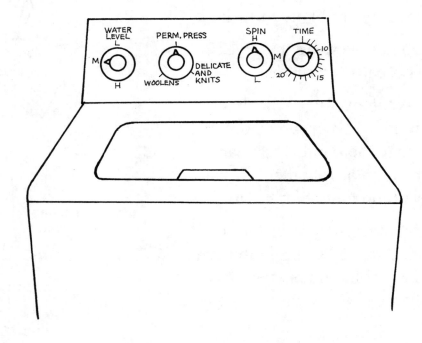

www.walch.com

Drying Clothes

Items you wash together in a load can be dried together, too. Before you put items into the dryer, shake them out.

If the items are mostly all-cotton, use the regular cycle. Items that are permanent press should be dried on the permanent press cycle. Some items should have only a brief tumble in the dryer, then be hung up.

Be sure to clean the lint trap after each use. Otherwise lint can build up and become a fire hazard.

Here are some more guidelines for drying clothes:

- Read the label before you dry. Some things should not go in the dryer at all.

- Sort clothes. Heavy fabrics such as jeans and towels need normal heat. Lightweight fabrics should be dried on low heat.

- Do not overdry fabrics. If you do, they are likely to shrink.

- Do not overload the dryer. This causes wrinkles.

- Take items out of the dryer right away when they are dry. Shake them out. Then hang them up or fold them. If you wait too long, they'll wrinkle.

- If you line-dry your fabrics, hang white fabrics in the sun. Hang colored items in the shade.

Washer and Dryer Safety

Here are a few safety rules to follow when using your
washer and dryer:

- Never put fabric containing paint, wax, or gas in a washer
  or dryer. Wash the fabric out by hand first. Be sure the
  paint, wax, or gas is gone before putting the item in the
  dryer. Fumes could cause an explosion in the dryer.

- Store all detergents, bleach, and other cleaning products out
  of the reach of children.

- Locate the dryer's lint trap. It may be inside the door or
  on top of the machine. Always clean the lint trap on the
  dryer before each use. Don't let lint pile up under the dryer,
  either. This could cause a fire.

- Don't dry items containing plastic or rubber in the dryer.
  Hang these items outside to dry.

- If you have a gas dryer and smell gas, open the window.
  Don't light a match. Don't turn lights on or off. Leave the
  house if the smell is strong. Call the gas company from
  a neighbor's house.

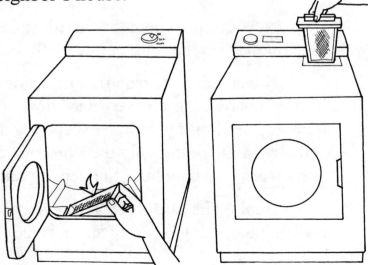

www.walch.com

Using an Iron

If you take many items right out of the dryer when they're dry, you won't have to iron them at all. This is the best plan!

But many fabrics will need ironing to look their best. Before you start, read the label to see what type of fabric you are ironing. Then set the iron for the right temperature.

If you want to use steam, unplug the iron, then add water. Steam ironing often makes ironing easier.

Sort items that need ironing by the amount of heat needed. Some fabrics such as silks or synthetics require a low ironing temperature. Cottons and linens need a higher temperature.

How do you know what temperature to use? First read the label on the clothing item to see what type of fabric it is. Then look on the control settings on the iron. It will tell you where to set the iron for the best results.

If you are ironing a shirt, iron the smaller parts first. This means that you should do the collar, cuffs, and sleeves first. Then do the body of the shirt.

Never iron an item that is still stained. If you do, you may set the stain permanently in the item.

Never leave the iron face down on the ironing board. Don't leave it face down on the item you are ironing, either, except when you are actually ironing—moving the iron back and forth. Otherwise, you may burn the item or cause a fire.

Unplug the iron when you're done. Let it cool on the ironing board or stove, standing on end.

Check Yourself

Write TRUE or FALSE on the line before each statement that follows. If the statement is false, explain why.

_____ 1. All things that are made of fabric can be washed in the washing machine.

_____ 2. Sort clothes by color before washing.

_____ 3. You can save money by washing fabrics the right way.

_____ 4. Ironing a stain makes it easier to get the stain out.

_____ 5. Store clean wool items in sealed plastic bags or boxes during the summer.

www.walch.com

_____   6. Detergent works in any water temperature.

_____   7. Soap works best in cold water.

_____   8. Bleach can remove many stains.

_____   9. Pour bleach directly on stained fabric.

_____   10. Lightweight fabrics should be dried on high heat.

_____   11. Overdrying fabric may cause it to shrink.

Continued ▶

_____ 12. If you hang your wash outside to dry, be sure to hang it in the sun.

_____ 13. Clean the lint trap on the dryer before each use.

_____ 14. You shouldn't dry plastic or rubber items in the dryer.

_____ 15. You can iron all fabrics with the same heat setting.

What Would You Do?

Tell what you would do in each case below.

1. You spill ketchup on your shirt.

2. Your brand-new orange shirt needs washing.

3. You want to do the least amount of ironing and still have your clothes look unwrinkled.

4. You want to wash some jeans that have gas spilled on them.

5. You have washed your bath rugs. They have rubber backing. How should you dry them?

6. You have a gas dryer. One day there is a strong smell of gas in the room. What should you do?

7. You are shopping for laundry detergent. How could you decide which kind to buy?

www.walch.com

Words to Know

ammonia	a cleaner that should never be mixed with bleach
appliance	an electrical machine for home use, such as a toaster or television
bleach	a chemical that whitens fabrics
circuit breaker	an electrical device that shuts off the flow of electricity
deadbolt lock	a strong type of lock in which the metal locking bar goes into the door frame
detergent	a good cleaner for washing clothes
disinfectant	a cleaner that kills germs
dry-clean	to clean with chemicals, not water
electrical fire	a fire involving an electrical appliance and/or electric current
electrical outlet	where electrical cords are plugged in
electrocuted	receiving an electric shock that can cause injury or death
evacuation plan	a plan to get out of a burning building safely
extension cord	an electrical cord that adds length to the original cord
fabric	cloth or material
fabric softener	a product added to rinse water to soften clothes
fire extinguisher	a device for putting out a small fire
flammable	able to catch fire easily
food poisoning	a sickness caused by bacteria in food

grease fire	oil or grease that catches fire
kindling	small sticks used to start a fire
lint screen	a screen on a dryer that catches excess lint to be removed
non-skid backing	rubber backing that holds a rug in place
outlet	where electrical cords are plugged in
poison	any substance that is harmful to the body
Poison Control Center	a place that gives advice in case of poisoning
smoke detector	a warning device that sounds an alarm in case of fire
space heater	a small, often portable, heater that heats one area of the house with direct heat
starch	a product used to make clothes crisper when ironed
toxic	deadly
UL label	Underwriters Laboratories label; a label that states that the appliance has been tested and is safe
water conditioner	a product added to hard water to make it soft

www.walch.com